THE OFFICIAL
Everton
FOOTBALL CLUB ANNUAL 2009

Written by Darren Griffiths, Matthew Gamble, Craig Davies and Adam Clark

Everton

A Grange Publication

© 2008. Published by Grange Communications Ltd., Edinburgh under licence from Everton Football Club. Printed in the EU.

ISBN 978-1-906211-32-5

Photographs © Action Images

£6.99

Everton

Contents

David Moyes

The Everton manager David Moyes thoroughly enjoyed the European adventure last season.

The Toffees played ten UEFA Cup ties and won eight of them, which is a terrific record. They drew one (at home to Metalist Kharkiv when they missed two penalties) and only lost to Italian side, Fiorentina.

It was a great return that probably deserved to carry the team further than the last 16 of the competition.

"We really enjoyed it, the supporters really enjoyed it and I think we were good for Europe," said Moyes.

"To say I loved it wouldn't be too strong a word - it might not be strong enough! I have loved it and I think we needed it. I needed it for my development, I think the players needed it and the Club needed it more than anybody.

"The games were very good and brought great excitement for the Goodison crowd as well as some great games away from home. Sadly it all culminated in us going out on penalties but at least it was on an outstanding night of football."

Ironically, one of the teams that Everton defeated actually went on to win the UEFA Cup!

Zenit St Petersberg were beaten 1-0 at Goodison during the Group stage but they recovered to go all the way and win the final against Glasgow Rangers at Manchester City's Eastlands Stadium.

"I watched the final with a little bit of disappointment that we weren't in it," admitted the Blues boss.

"But you have to earn the right and have a little bit of luck along the way."

Everton qualified for the UEFA Cup again by finishing 5th in the Premier League table at the end of the 2007/08 campaign and Moyes claimed that it was something his players thoroughly deserved.

"It was a nice way to end the season," he said. "The players did well from the first game to the last. We pushed really hard to try and finish fourth but we just fell short so it was important to finish fifth. It makes me smile that we have got more European nights to come."

"We really enjoyed it, the supporters really enjoyed it and I think we were good for Europe."

AUGUST

The kick off to the 2007/08 campaign brought the usual fervour and excitement.

Everton were back in Europe and the signings of Phil Jagielka from Sheffield United, Leighton Baines from Wigan and Steven Pienaar on loan from Borussia Dortmund meant the Toffees were better prepared for the season ahead than ever.

The opening game of the Premier League campaign ended with a 2-1 win over Chris Hutchings' Wigan – the second successive season the Toffees had hit the ground running. Leon Osman headed our first goal of the campaign before Victor Anichebe's second-half strike ensured Antoine Sibierski's late effort was nothing more than a consolation.

Things got even better as Everton returned from London three days later having recorded a memorable 3-1 victory over Martin Jol's much-fancied Tottenham, courtesy of goals from Joleon Lescott, Alan Stubbs and Osman.

Another away trip – this time to Reading's Madejski Stadium – resulted in the first defeat of the season. Midfielder Stephen Hunt scored the only goal of the game, but the Royals rode their luck as both James McFadden and Andrew Johnson hit the woodwork late on.

The final match of the opening month of the campaign ended all square...but Everton needed a James McFadden equaliser to earn a point against Blackburn Rovers at Goodison.

With the transfer deadline looming David Moyes made a last-ditch move to bolster Everton's attack, bringing in Middlesbrough's Ayegbeni Yakubu for a club record fee of £11.25million. The signing excited the Goodison Park faithful and the Nigerian international would go on to prove their optimism was not misplaced...

Leon Osman celebrates after scoring at White Hart Lane against Tottenham

SEPTEMBER

It took 'The Yak' just 10 minutes to get off the mark, putting Everton in front at Bolton's Reebok Stadium. Partnering Andrew Johnson, the new-look attack combined brilliantly with the latter providing his new team-mate with the opportunity to announce his arrival with a well-taken goal.

Nicolas Anelka volleyed an equaliser early in the second half but Lescott popped up to head home a dramatic winner with just two minutes left on the clock.

Next up at Goodison were Manchester United, but anybody unaccustomed to the Premier League

Joleon Lescott secures a win at
Bolton with a last minute goal

would have been hard pushed to identify which
side were the reigning champions.

Everton – dogged, determined, defiant – looked
to have battled their way to a well-deserved
draw when, with just seven minutes to go,
Nemanja Vidic met Nani's corner to steal
all three points. It was especially tough on
goalkeeper Stefan Wessels who was making his
first appearance for the Blues since arriving
from German outfit FC Cologne.

The UEFA Cup campaign began in frustrating
fashion as Ukrainian side Metalist Kharkiv forced
a 1-1 draw at Goodison. All had looked rosy when
Lescott headed his third goal of the season
midway through the first half, but the Blues
went on to miss two penalties and concede
a late equaliser. All that and the
visitors had two men sent off!

Domestically, Everton's impressive
start to the campaign continued
as Sheffield Wednesday were
brushed aside in the Carling Cup
and Middlesbrough were defeated
in the league. A 2-0 defeat at Aston
Villa was the only glum note for
Moyes' men.

OCTOBER

Into October and following the excitement of
overcoming Metalist Kharkiv in the UEFA Cup
2nd leg, Everton were brought back down to
earth with defeat at Newcastle three days later.

The Toffees had looked good value for a 1-1 draw
following Johnson's strike but two goals in the
final four minutes swung the encounter in favour
of the hosts. Shay Given's injury-time own goal cut
the deficit but the Magpies held on for a 3-2 win.

Things were to get worse before they got better
as two Dirk Kuyt penalties gave Liverpool a highly
controversial 2-1 Mersey derby win at Goodison.

Sami Hyypia holds his head in his hands
after his own goal in the Goodison derby

9

The result was all the more upsetting as the first penalty – awarded for Tony Hibbert's 'foul' on Steven Gerrard – was highly debatable. Furthermore, Hibbert received a red card. He was later joined by Phil Neville who handled a goal-bound effort to give away the second spot kick.

The nine men of Everton were then denied a clear penalty in the dying seconds as Mark Clattenburg failed to spot Jamie Carragher dragging Joleon Lescott to the ground.

The UEFA Cup provided the perfect opportunity to bounce back as Greek side Larissa travelled to Merseyside. Everton were dominant throughout and won the opening Group game 3-1.

Trips to newly-promoted Derby County and Carling Cup fourth round opponents Luton Town provided two successive victories as the Blues went into November in fine fettle.

NOVEMBER

Birmingham were the next side to succumb to Moyes' confident troops as Lee Carsley and James Vaughan struck in injury time to secure a richly-deserved 3-1 win. To add to the delight it was a fourth straight victory for the Toffees – a feat which had not been achieved for 13 years.

The dramatic European adventure continued as goals from Arteta and Anichebe in the final 10 minutes added consecutive win number five in Nürnberg.

Extending the run further looked an uphill challenge however as a trip to Stamford Bridge was next on the agenda. But the Blues hustled and bustled and got their reward when Cahill's spectacular 89th-minute overhead kick earned a 1-1 draw.

Yakubu finds the net during the 7-1 win over Sunderland

Yakubu's last-gasp winner sends Everton through to the Carling Cup semi-finals

It got even better! The visit of Roy Keane's Sunderland inspired a flamboyant display that will live long in the memory of Evertonians.

Yakubu began the rout, his shot looping over goalkeeper Craig Gordon courtesy of a deflection, Cahill quickly added a second, Pienaar fired a classy third and although Dwight Yorke handed Sunderland a lifeline before the break, Cahill's second soon restored the three-goal advantage.

Yakubu added a fifth before departing the field for Andrew Johnson who wasted no time in joining the goalscorers' party to make it six. And it didn't stop there. There was still time for Osman to wade through the Black Cats' rearguard and stroke home another. Everton 7 Sunderland 1.

DECEMBER

A busy December began with a goalless draw at Portsmouth - a notable achievement against a side notoriously tough to beat on home soil.

Moyes' boys then welcomed Zenit St Petersburg and sent the future UEFA Cup winners packing courtesy of a Cahill strike six minutes from time. The 1-0 victory not only booked Everton's place in the last 32 of the competition but ensured they would progress as group winners.

Yakubu's first hat-trick for the club - and the first by an Everton player in four years - saw the Toffees swagger their way to another three-point haul. This time Fulham were the side to depart Goodison on the wrong end of a defeat.

A double-header with West Ham United followed and Everton came out the other side with three more league points and a place in the Carling Cup semi-finals - a stage of the competition they had not reached for two decades.

Everton then preserved their 100% winning record in Group A of the UEFA Cup with a 3-2 success at AZ Alkmaar. It was a club record seventh consecutive away win in cup competitions and Jack Rodwell became the youngest player to turn out for the Blues in Europe.

The result also stretched the club's unbeaten run to 13 games. And, typically, it was to prove unlucky.

Confronted with a trip to Old Trafford, Everton put in another valiant display against the future European Champions only to have a point snatched away late on when Cristiano Ronaldo made it 2-1 from the penalty spot.

And although the Blues recovered well to beat Bolton on Boxing Day the year ended with a thumping 4-1 defeat at home to Arsenal.

Player Interview

Steven Pienaar

Steven Pienaar learned to play football by kicking a tennis ball in the streets of Johannesburg, in South Africa.

The small boy who would go on to represent his country and star in the English Premier League honed his skills in the most basic fashion.

"I used to play with a tennis ball in the street with my friends," he said. "If we were lucky, someone would have a proper football.

"When I was about 8 I started to play for a local Under-12s team. I was always the smallest in the team because we didn't have an Under-10s. But playing with older and bigger guys helped me to develop as a footballer and it was good for me."

At the age of 15 he had perfected his ability so much that he was invited to Holland for a trial with the world famous Ajax team.

"There were a lot of players in my position and so they sent me back home to play for one of their feeder clubs, Ajax Cape Town," he explained.

"I actually got a scholarship to go to the USA to study and play soccer but I turned it down because I wasn't into studying. I did well for Ajax Cape Town for six months and then got the call to go back to Amsterdam.

"I was really excited about it because it had been my dream to play overseas. I always wanted to play in Holland because of the style of play over there."

Steven made his debut for Ajax at the age of 19 and he later played for the team in the quarter-finals of the European Champions League.

In January 2006, Steven left Ajax to sign for German club Borussia Dortmund but he never really settled in his new surroundings.

"Going to Dortmund was a tough decision but I learned a lot and it made me even stronger," he said. "I was very much by myself and I had to settle in. It was a good experience but there was no time to adjust."

Things never really worked out for the midfielder in Germany and he was happy when he got the opportunity to come to England and join Everton.

"The move to Everton came something out of the blue," he said. "But I got a good feeling straight away. All the guys were friendly and made me feel at home from the first day. That always makes you happy and makes you want to do your best for the team.

"The whole squad are friendly. I've never met a group of players like them! They want to help and there are a lot of characters."

"All the guys were friendly and made me feel at home from the first day. That always makes you happy and makes you want to do your best for the team."

Awards Event

Everton's third annual End of Season Awards took place at St George's Hall in May 2008.

David Moyes and his first team squad were joined at the glittering affair by a whole host of legends from the Club's illustrious past.

All were at the show-piece city centre venue to witness the presentation of a series of prizes to top performers and notable achievers during the 2007/08 season.

The big winner on the night was Joleon Lescott, who not only won the Supporters' Player of the Year, but also the highly regarded Players' Player of the Year award.

The awards underlined Lescott's growing stature as an Everton player.

"I got the Players' Player prize last season but to get the award from the fans this year is fantastic," said Lescott. "It is a great privilege and I am sure the awards will take pride of place at my parents' house - they will be looking to get hold of them.

"It has been a good season for me, but it has been a good season for the whole team and it is all about the team here at Everton. They are a great bunch of lads."

Victor Anichebe followed in the footsteps of best friend James Vaughan by winning the Young Player of the Season Award while Leon Osman's beautifully crafted goal against Larissa in Europe was deemed to be Everton's Goal of the Season.

Osman was presented with the award by former Blues striker Graeme Sharp, and was delighted to accept it.

He said: "It's very pleasing. It's the first award I have won and it's a privilege. There was a big team effort involved and I was there to finish it off.

"There were some good goals in there and I'm delighted to have won it."

Goalkeeping legend Gordon West was named as the Everton Giant for 2008 and the Howard Kendall Award went to the Everton Ladies team for their efforts in securing two trophies and a second place finish in the FA Women's Premier League.

The Fan of the Year was Terry Parker, who has been supporting Everton home and away since World War II. Aged 73, he goes to every single home game and makes nearly every away trip too!

Junior quiz

Answers on page 61

1 From which club did Everton sign Leighton Baines?

2 With which Scottish club did David Moyes make his debut as a player?

3 Who knocked Everton out of last season's FA Cup?

4 Who left Everton last season to become the manager of Preston North End?

5 What job does Mick Rathbone do at Everton?

6 Everton goalkeeping coach, Chris Woods, played for which country as an international?

7 James McFadden joined which club when he left Everton?

8 For which country does Steven Pienaar play his international football?

9 What stand at Goodison is directly opposite the Park End?

10 Which Liverpool player scored an own goal in last season's derby match at Goodison?

11 Which team did Everton defeat 8-1 on aggregate in last season's UEFA Cup?

12 Everton defeated Luton Town, West Ham and which other team to reach last season's Carling Cup semi-final?

Get Everton in your pocket!

You can now get Everton Mobile any place, any time! With the new Everton WAP site you can now access the latest news, ticket info and fantastic downloads from your mobile phone.

For a link to the site, text EVERTON to 61718*

Choose from wallpapers, animations, videos and much, much more to show your allegiance to the Blues!

WALLPAPERS

Support Everton with the latest Blue backgrounds. Choose from match action pictures, Everton legends, stadium shots, official club crests and first-team player images.

CUSTOMISED SHIRTS

Get your name and number on the back of an Everton shirt and have it sent to your mobile as a wallpaper.

VIDEOS

Get the latest highlights direct to your mobile. Choose from goals, interviews, archived classic match highlights and, of course, current Premier League action!

RINGTONES

Get your mobile bouncing with the latest Evertonian chants, real tones, polyphonics and more.

GAMES

Get official Everton games straight to your mobile and take your pick from the best of the rest.

TEXT ALERTS

Stay in touch with Everton wherever you are. Get the latest news, scores and match updates straight to your mobile.

ASK SHARPY

Let Graeme Sharp and his team answer all your Everton related questions within minutes!

REVERSE AUCTION

Everton Reverse Auction is our fantastic reverse auction prize competition, where the LOWEST UNIQUE BID wins, not the highest. Bid by text or on our website for the chance to win incredible prizes for pennies!

Please ensure your mobile is WAP enabled. Standard network rates apply.

Finch Farm Training Complex

Everton moved training grounds during the 2007/08 season!

The brand new site at Finch Farm, in the south of the city, was completed in September 2007 and David Moyes moved in with his players the following month.

The state of the art complex replaced the old Bellefield training site and it is big enough to house the senior professionals as well as the club's Academy.

It is the first time everyone has been under the same roof.

Development of the site took 150 weeks including pitch construction and landscaping. It was a massive undertaking, with 69,000 ceramic tiles, 68,000 concrete blocks, 4,376 carpet tiles, 550 tins of paint, 265 tonnes of steel and 1,400 cubic metres of concrete used on a building that boasts 6,410 square-metres of space for the Academy and first team to utilise.

Wordsearch

EVERTON FA CUP HEROES

Look at the grid below - can you spot the names of 15 Everton FA Cup heroes?

D	D	N	U	N	S	W	O	R	T	H	W	Y
X	E	E	B	F	D	M	S	E	L	G	M	Q
R	K	N	A	K	C	D	M	H	G	H	I	N
A	T	K	O	N	N	P	P	M	E	H	K	M
T	R	R	J	B	L	B	L	C	C	E	S	Q
C	E	N	Y	E	A	G	R	A	Y	A	D	R
L	B	O	E	X	M	L	K	L	G	K	K	Y
I	I	S	V	R	Q	O	P	A	C	X	M	M
F	L	T	R	X	M	R	R	D	R	M	B	J
F	C	A	A	A	A	X	T	X	F	T	Y	B
E	O	W	H	H	T	U	O	E	D	I	R	R
F	C	M	S	X	R	V	H	C	H	N	R	M
T	K	Q	K	L	L	A	H	T	U	O	S	J

AMOKACHI   RATCLIFFE   SOUTHALL

DEAN   RIDEOUT   TEMPLE

GRAY   SAGAR   TREBILCOCK

HARVEY   SHARP   UNSWORTH

LABONE   SHEEDY   WATSON

Answers on page 61

Everton Tigers

The Everton Tigers was officially presented as the 13th member of the British Basketball League in June 2007.

The Blues teamed up with the Toxteth Tigers to form a new basketball club that compete in the British Basketball League.

The club continues to operate on the community platform generated from the Toxteth Tigers programme that has enjoyed success from a grass roots level right up to international standard for over 40 years.

The Tigers are very much a part of the Everton family (The Toffees became the fifth football club in the history of British basketball to field a basketball team, following in the footsteps of Manchester United, Glasgow Rangers, Portsmouth and Newcastle United) and the Head Coach for the 2008/09 season is Tony Garbelotto, who has also coached the England international team.

The Tigers home stadium is the Greenbank Sports Centre in the south of Liverpool, although during last season they played Cheshire Jets at the Echo Arena and attracted a crowd in excess of 6,000.

The squad, which includes international stars such as Chris Haslam and Richard Midgley, was presented to the Goodison Park crowd during the half-time interval in a UEFA Cup match.

At the end of their first competitive season in the British Basketball League, Everton Tigers finished in 7th position in the table. This was enough to see them reach the play-offs but they were beaten by Guilford Heat, 81-72.

'The Tigers are very much a part of the Everton family – The Toffees became the fifth football club in the history of British basketball to field a basketball team.'

21

Legends

Evertonians like nothing better than watching the goals fly into the net at Goodison Park and the fans have been lucky over the years to have seen some of the best centre forwards around.

The immortal Dixie Dean set the standards for everyone else to follow and although the great man's goalscoring record is highly unlikely to ever be surpassed, these striking heroes have certainly given the supporters plenty to cheer about....

TONY COTTEE
240 APPS 99 GOALS

KEVIN CAMPBELL
164 APPS 51 GOALS

BOB LATCHFORD
289 APPS 138 GOALS

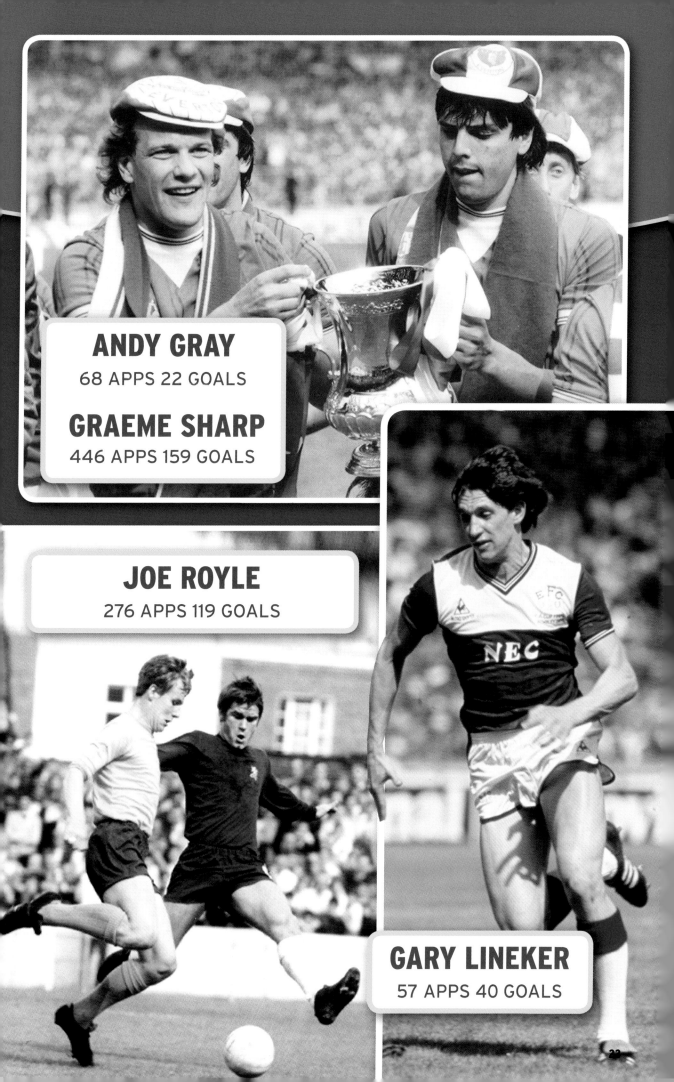

ANDY GRAY
68 APPS 22 GOALS

GRAEME SHARP
446 APPS 159 GOALS

JOE ROYLE
276 APPS 119 GOALS

GARY LINEKER
57 APPS 40 GOALS

Player profiles

IAIN TURNER

Highly-rated keeper Iain arrived at Goodison in January 2003 in a £50,000 deal from Stirling Albion.

He was much in-demand with Premier League clubs Tottenham and Charlton also rumoured to be interested. But it was David Moyes who swooped to sign him following a successful three-day trial.

And the Scotland under-21 international has continued to impress since making his debut as a late replacement for the injured Richard Wright in a 4-1 FA Cup fourth round defeat to Chelsea at Stamford Bridge in February 2006.

In the spring of 2007 Iain moved to Sheffield Wednesday on loan and it proved a hugely successful move. He remained unbeaten during his 11-game spell with The Owls and manager Brian Laws made no secret of his desire to sign him permanently.

But his value to Everton was underlined when he was offered a new contract to keep him at Goodison until 2011. His talents didn't go unnoticed by his country either and Iain received his first call-up to the senior Scotland squad for the Euro 2008 qualifiers.

TIM HOWARD

Since joining Everton from Manchester United in the summer of 2006 Tim has gone from strength to strength.

Originally arriving on loan, the American international made such an impression that in February 2007 the deal was made permanent for an undisclosed fee.

He began his career playing for the New York/New Jersey Metrostars, where he eventually replaced USA international keeper Tony Meola as the first choice in goal.

He then moved to United in 2003 and made 77 appearances before falling behind Edwin van der Sar in the pecking order. United's loss was Everton's gain.

A finger injury sustained on international duty disrupted Tim's early 2007/08 season with the goalkeeper missing four games, including one against his former team.

But once he returned he enjoyed an excellent season. Ever reliable and regularly producing excellent saves, he was one short of equalling Neville Southall's record of 15 clean sheets in a league season.

JOHN RUDDY

John joined Everton from Cambridge United in the summer of 2005, for a fee of £250,000.

He had made 39 appearances in League Two after making his professional debut at the age of 18.

Loan spells at Walsall and Chester gave John valuable first-team experience before he made his Everton debut in unusual circumstances in February 2006.

Third choice keeper Iain Turner started the game against Blackburn but was dismissed after just eight minutes for handball outside the box. John was thrust into the fray and managed to keep a clean sheet in a 1-0 Everton victory.

Further loan spells at Stockport County, Wrexham and Bristol City followed and in the 2007/08 season, the youngster was an unused sub in the Premier League on a number of occasions.

A return to Stockport saw John win the League Two player of the month award for March 2008 - keeping five clean sheets in six games.

TONY HIBBERT

Considered by many to be Everton's best tackler, Academy graduate Tony has become a key part of David Moyes' squad. Originally a midfield player, the Liverpool-born star has combined excellent defensive qualities with intelligent running to adapt well to the right-back position in recent seasons.

A member of the Toffees 1998 FA Youth Cup winning side, Tony made his debut in March 2001 as Everton defeated West Ham 2-0 at Upton Park.

The lifelong Blue was rewarded for his committed performances with a new contract in January 2003 and then again in 2005. Hibbert shared right-back duties with Phil Neville in the first part of the 2007/08 campaign, performing in typically reliable fashion. He signed another new deal in January 2008 which will keep him at Everton until the summer of 2012. The tenacious tackler was an important figure in the second half of the campaign, turning in a series of typically sturdy performances.

LEIGHTON BAINES

Leighton joined Everton just a few days before the start of the 2007/08 campaign. Recruited from Wigan Athletic for an undisclosed fee, the defender signed on for five seasons.

Having been on the Toffees' books as a teenager, Leighton eventually joined Wigan's youth scheme and made his senior debut at the age of 17. He went on to make nearly 150 appearances for the Latics, impressing in the Premier League and becoming a regular for England under-21s.

An attacking and tenacious left-back, Leighton was a vital player for both his club and country, playing all England's games in the 2007 Euro under-21 Championships.

He missed the first few games of the 2007/08 season through injury but impressed on his return, sharing left-back duties with Joleon Lescott and Nuno Valente.

Player profiles

JOSEPH YOBO

Joseph joined the Blues in the summer of 2002, declining offers from Arsenal and Juventus, to become David Moyes' first signing.

He signed a 12-month contract with the Blues, with an option for a further four years, which was taken up by Moyes in November 2002.

Good in the air, strong in the tackle and difficult to hassle off the ball, the defender also possesses tremendous vision - attributes which helped him win Everton's Young Player of the Year Award for the 2003/04 season.

He signed a long-term five year contract in the summer of 2006 and went on to play every minute of every Premiership game during the 2006/07 season, matching a record last achieved 20 years earlier by Kevin Ratcliffe.

He was a vital part in the Blues defence throughout the 2007/08 campaign and notched his only goal of the season in the 2-2 draw with Aston Villa in April...before scoring twice for Nigeria in the African Cup of Nations qualifiers in the summer!

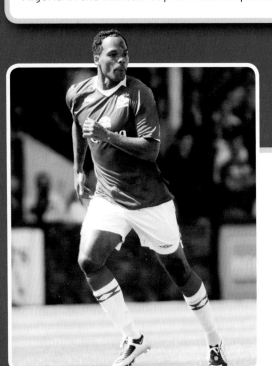

JOLEON LESCOTT

Joleon signed for Everton in June 2006, joining from Championship side Wolverhampton Wanderers for an undisclosed fee. Born in Birmingham, the versatile defender progressed through the Centre of Excellence at Wolves, making his first-team debut when he was 18 years old. He went on to make 224 appearances for the Midlanders, scoring 13 goals.

An instant hit at Goodison, Joleon played in every match of his first season, winning the Players' Player of the Year accolade. He was linked with clubs such as Real Madrid and Chelsea such was his impact, and in October 2007 his form earned him an England debut against Estonia.

The popular defender agreed a new contract in March 2008, which will keep him at Goodison Park until at least the summer of 2012.

Joleon's performances in 2007/08 earned him the Player of the Season and Players' Player of the Season awards, and a goal against Newcastle on the final day of the season meant he finished with 10 for the campaign.

PHIL JAGIELKA

Phil Jagielka joined Everton from Sheffield United in the summer of 2007 in a deal worth £4million. A versatile performer, he can play in central defence, full back and also in midfield.

He is also a capable goalkeeper and was called into action for the Blades on several occasions, most notably when he kept a clean sheet in a 1-0 home win over Arsenal in the 2006/07 season!

Jags, who was at Everton's Academy for a period in his teens, made his Toffees debut as a substitute against Tottenham in a 3-1 win at White Hart Lane in August 2007.

But it wasn't until Joseph Yobo's involvement in the African Cup of Nations in January 2008 that he got a chance to truly shine. He grasped it with both hands, forging a strong partnership with Joleon Lescott and later the returning Yobo. His performances caught the eye of England manager Fabio Capello and he was handed his international debut in a friendly against Trinidad and Tobago.

NUNO VALENTE

Nuno arrived at Goodison Park from Porto days before the transfer window closed in August 2005. A Champions League winner in 2004, he played under Jose Mourinho whilst at Estadio do Dragao and the former Chelsea manager spoke to David Moyes ahead of his transfer, highly recommending him. Noted for the quality of his crossing and the venom of his shot, Nuno improved rapidly at Everton in his first campaign.

His second campaign was blighted by injury however and he barely featured after Christmas due to a succession of niggling problems.

The Portuguese international again endured a disjointed campaign in 2007/08, but was able to feature in the 7-1 win over Sunderland and the 2-0 win in Nürnberg.

And despite his problems, Everton's faith was highlighted when they activated a one-year extension to his contract to keep him at Goodison until summer 2009.

DAN GOSLING

Dan signed for the Blues during the 2008 January transfer window. The youngster arrived on Merseyside from Plymouth Argyle, where he had made his professional debut aged just 16.

Predominantly right-sided, Dan can play both in defence and midfield and has been involved with the England under-17 and under-18 sides. Touted by David Moyes as one for the future, the youngster slotted well into Andy Holden's reserve side and was soon training with the first team. He was an unused substitute for the UEFA Cup tie against Fiorentina in Italy and also occupied the bench on the final day against Newcastle. Dan was also part of England's squad for the 2008 European under-17 Championships in the Czech Republic.

Player profiles

JOHN IRVING

Local lad John is a speedy defender who is comfortable at either centre back or full back. He has been a model of consistency for Andy Holden's reserve side and was named Reserve Player of the Year for 2006/07 after being given the captain's armband in February 2007.

His ability and reliability has been acknowledged at international level, with appearances for England under-16s and he was an unused substitute for Everton's UEFA Cup match against AZ Alkmaar.
A second-string regular, John won the Reserve Player of the Season award for the second year in a row and he was further rewarded with a one-year contract in the summer of 2008.

JACK RODWELL

Jack is a record-breaking youngster, after making his full Everton debut as a substitute against Alkmaar at the age of just 16 years and 284 days to become the youngest ever Toffees player to play in Europe.

The Southport-born defender, who can also play in midfield, is used to making debuts at a young age. He was just 15 when he made his first reserve appearance, replacing David Weir in a game with Sheffield United in October 2006. A year earlier, at the age of 14, Jack made his Everton under-18s debut.

A highly-rated prospect, Jack has also gained international recognition. He earned five caps for England's under-16 team, and captained the side to glory in the Victory Shield in December 2006. He has since progressed to captain the under-18s.

In March 2008, he appeared as a substitute at Sunderland - his Premier League debut - before also featuring as a replacement in the final game of the season.

JOHN PAUL KISSOCK

After joining the Academy, JP impressed immediately, becoming a regular with the under-18s and the reserve side. A fleet-footed midfielder, he also has excellent vision and a strength that belies his small stature. His performances caught the eye of the international selectors as he was placed on stand-by for the England under-19 squad. John Paul was called up to the first-team squad ahead of the game in Alkmaar but did not make the substitutes bench. However, his regular appearances in the reserve side mean he is knocking on the door for first team recognition. In January 2008, JP joined SPL side Gretna on loan for the remainder of the season. Despite the club enduring a difficult end to the campaign, Kissock caught the eye with some gutsy showings.

MIKEL ARTETA

Mikel began his career with Barcelona at the age of 15 before moving to Paris Saint-Germain FC in 2000. Rangers brought him to Glasgow two years later and he was part of the team that won the Scottish Premier League, Scottish Cup and Scottish League Cup in 2003.

However, injury and loss of form curtailed his progress and he moved back to Spain with Real Sociedad. The versatile and skilful midfielder struggled to hold down a regular place at La Real however and Everton swooped to sign him on loan in January 2005. The playmaker impressed with a host of classy displays and a £2million permanent deal was concluded in July 2005. His debut season ended with Mikel being named Everton's Player of the Season as well as the Players' Player of the Season. His good form continued into the 2006/07 campaign and not only was he awarded with another Player of the Year trophy but also a new five-year contract. And he again proved his worth in the 2007/08 season helping Everton secure fifth-place in the Premier League.

ANDY VAN DER MEYDE

Andy became Everton's eighth signing of a hectic summer in 2005 when he arrived from Inter Milan on transfer deadline day. He put pen to paper on a four year contract with the Blues - a deal set to keep him at Goodison until the age of 29. The pacy winger began his career with hometown club Vitesse Arnhem before moving on to Ajax and later Inter.

Unfortunately for the likeable Dutchman, he managed only 11 appearances for the Blues in his debut season. Injury, and later suspension, meant he found it difficult to make a mark on the Premier League.

He did show flashes of the flair and skill that he undoubtedly possesses and proved highly popular with the Goodison Park faithful. But that flair was all too fleeting during a 2006/07 season that was, once again, marred by injury and loss of form. The 2007/08 campaign started in similar fashion and the unfortunate winger never managed to get closer than a place on the substitutes bench throughout the season - largely due to injuries.

TIM CAHILL

So determined was Tim to forge a career in professional football that he left behind family and friends in Australia at the age of 16, travelling halfway round the world to try his luck in England. His determination and courage has certainly been well rewarded.

A forceful, strong-running midfielder, he is remarkably good in the air for a player of only average height and after 250 appearances for Millwall (including the 2004 FA Cup final) he earned a 'dream' move to Everton.

His first season in the Premier League saw him win the Player of the Season award at Goodison after finishing the campaign as top scorer.

He was once again a key figure for the side during the 2005/06 campaign and earned a call up to the World Cup with Australia. Cahill returned to Everton and began the 2006/07 season in sensational style, bagging seven goals before the end of October. Injuries hampered the rest of his season but his importance to the club was highlighted by a five-year contract extension. A memorable overhead kick against Chelsea was his personal highlight of 2007/08 and although he again missed chunks of the campaign Tim finished with 10 goals.

Player profiles

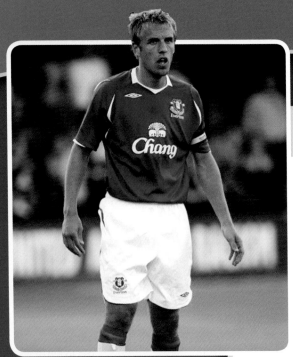

PHIL NEVILLE

England international Phil arrived at Goodison from Manchester United in August 2005.

Renowned for his versatility, the younger of the two Neville brothers brought a wealth of European and international experience to Moyes' side. Interestingly, Phil's sporting career could have taken a very different path. At the age of 14 he had to make the choice between football and cricket, having excelled as a young player at Lancashire Cricket Club where he broke batting records set by Mike Atherton. Cricket's loss was football's gain.

Capable of operating as left or right-back or in the midfield, Phil has become a key member of the Everton squad and took over the club captaincy from David Weir in January 2007.

A consummate professional, he was a virtual ever-present during his first season with the Blues and again in 2006/07 and 2007/08.

STEVEN PIENAAR

Steven joined Everton in the summer of 2007 on loan from Borussia Dortmund.

After a successful season the midfielder's long-term future soon became a topic of debate. But Everton eventually concluded a permanent deal in April 2008, securing the South African's services for three years. Steven emerged as one of the hottest talents in the game whilst playing for Dutch giants Ajax. He excelled during his time in Amsterdam and was part of a side that contained Zlatan Ibrahimovic and Andy van der Meyde.

His Toffees career began brightly and he quickly became an integral part of the midfield with his creativity a vital part of Everton's attacking play. He didn't take long to get off the mark either, scoring his first goal for the Blues in a 2-0 victory against Middlesbrough in September.

He played for South Africa at the 2008 African Cup of Nations in Ghana, but returned in time to help Moyes' men secure fifth-place in the Premier League.

LEON OSMAN

Leon has risen through the ranks at Everton to become a real fans' favourite.

His dreams of becoming a professional footballer were almost shattered in 2001 when he suffered a serious knee injury that kept him out of action for almost a year, but he has bounced back in style.

A midfielder who combines excellent passing and vision with an eye for goal, he forced his way into David Moyes' first-team plans after loan spells at Carlisle United and Derby County.

He made his first start for the Toffees against Wolves in May 2004, scoring his first goal for the club after just three minutes.

Leon became a first-team regular during the 2004/05 season and was rewarded with a new long-term contract. He then cemented his place with a strong showing in the 2005/06 season and another in the following campaign. In 2007/08 he won Everton's Goal of the Season for a stunning long-range strike against Greek outfit Larissa.

LUKAS JUTKIEWICZ

Lukas Jutkiewicz arrived at Everton from Swindon Town in the summer of 2007.

He agreed a deal in March of that year after emerging as one of the hottest young prospects in the lower divisions. Lukas made his senior bow for Swindon in April 2006 when he was just 17 and scored his first ever goal at Walsall's Bescott Stadium that December.

He helped the Robins gain promotion to League One at the end of the 2006/07 campaign and left the club having made 13 starts and 20 substitute appearances. He scored five goals in that time.

Lukas was named on the Everton bench during the 2007/08 UEFA Cup campaign and later joined Championship side Plymouth Argyle on loan. The youngster made one start and two substitute appearances for the Pilgrims before returning to Finch Farm.

JAMES VAUGHAN

Striker James has been at Everton since the age of nine.

He was spotted by the Blues' talent scouts while playing in the Preston area and has risen all the way through the ranks to the first team. James' 73rd-minute substitute appearance against Crystal Palace on April 10, 2005, ensured that the Birmingham-born youngster broke Joe Royle's record as the club's youngest first-team player. He was just 16 years and 271 days old! Then his 84th-minute strike not only made him Everton's youngest-ever scorer, surpassing Wayne Rooney, but he also overtook James Milner as the Premiership's youngest scorer. James was rewarded with his first professional contract in the summer of 2005 but a succession of injuries hampered his progress. He returned to the fold in 2006/07, netting three times in six games at the end of the season. It was enough to earn him the club's Young Player of the Season award and a new four-year deal. Injuries again disrupted James' 2007/08 campaign but he did manage two goals in 13 appearances.

Player profiles

AYEGBENI YAKUBU

Yakubu joined Everton for a club record fee of £11.25 million in August 2007.

The striker switched from Middlesbrough to Merseyside and made himself an instant hit, becoming the first Everton player to score 20 goals in a season since Peter Beardsley in 1992. The Nigerian international shot to fame at Portsmouth where he scored 29 Premier League goals in just 68 games. He later made the move north to the Riverside and helped spearhead Boro into the UEFA Cup final in 2006.

Nicknamed The Yak, he is a powerful striker and his Everton career got off to a flying start when he scored on his debut against Bolton Wanderers. He remained a constant scoring threat throughout the season, notching a career best 21 goals – a haul that included hat tricks against Fulham and SK Brann. Yak also found time to participate in the African Cup of Nations, helping Nigeria to the quarter-finals.

VICTOR ANICHEBE

Victor is a powerful, pacy striker born in Nigeria who is a product of the Everton Academy.

He made his senior debut as a substitute in an FA Cup fourth-round tie against Chelsea at Goodison in January 2006. And his first goal for the club came on the final day of the same season, when he scored in the 2-2 draw against West Brom after coming on as a late substitute. The 2006/07 season saw Victor truly establish himself as a regular in the first-team squad and he was rewarded with a four-year contract.

He then continued his progression in 2007/08, most notably in Europe. Having scored on the opening day of the Premier League campaign, he went on to score four times in continental competition. In March 2008, he made his first appearance for Nigeria, scoring for the Super Eagles Olympic side in a qualifier against South Africa. He was subsequently voted Everton's Young Player of the Season by supporters.

JOSE BAXTER

Jose Baxter has been at Everton since he was just 6 years old!

Born in Liverpool in February 1992, he joined the Everton first-team squad that toured Switzerland and America during the pre-season... just two months after leaving school!

A player of immense natural talent he can perform in midfield or attack and has represented England at every age group up to Under-17s.

He scored his first goal for the senior team when he equalized at Nottingham Forest in a friendly match in July 2008.

Spot the difference

Can you spot 8 differences between these two pictures of Phil Jagielka in action against Fiorentina in the UEFA Cup?

ANSWERS ON PAGE 61

Player interview

Phil Jagielka

Phil Jagielka went from relegation to international within the space of 12 months!

The Blues defender was recruited following Sheffield United's drop into the Championship at the end of the 2006/07 season and his first campaign at Everton went so well that Fabio Capello gave him an England debut.

Jags played the second half of the 3-0 win against Trinidad & Tobago in June 2008 but was then alarmed to discover that the match was in danger of being declared as 'unofficial' by FIFA.

Had that been the case then he wouldn't have been awarded his first cap!

The problem was the number of substitutions made in the game. FIFA normally only allow six changes in international friendlies but England made seven.

"I would have been gutted if the game had been wiped out of the record books and I had been denied my first international cap," said Jags afterwards.

"It was a bit of a rollercoaster for me at the time. I was buzzing about getting my first cap and playing half the game but it was strange the next morning when I woke up and heard on the radio that FIFA weren't happy."

Thankfully, the game was sanctioned and Jags duly received his sparkling new cap from the Football Association.

He was now a real international footballer!

"It was a great experience for me and although it was a long time away at the end of a long season it was well worth it," he declared. "I was a bit nervous to begin with, but there were quite a few players in the same boat which made it easier."

Jags quickly settled down and enjoyed working alongside the cream of English football. He was also pleased to discover that not only were his new team-mates great footballers, but that they were really good guys too.

"Not only are the players first class, they are nice people off the pitch too," he said. "I was a bit nervous at first but I found it quite easy in the end. After all, I'm not the hardest person to talk to!"

His Everton team-mate, Phil Neville, certainly agrees with that last statement!

"He's not shy isn't Jags – his nicknames are microphone, amp or any other loud name!" laughed the Toffees captain.

"His character fits perfectly into this club and his performances have been outstanding."

Another team-mate quick to offer praise was goalkeeper Tim Howard.

"Jags is very much in the John Terry mould in that he blocks loads of shots," said Tim. "He's a no-nonsense player and takes care of the defensive side of things.

"He fully deserved his England call-up because there is no-one more consistent as a defender in the Premier League than Jags. He was absolutely outstanding this season."

"It was a bit of a rollercoaster for me at the time. I was buzzing about getting my first cap and playing half the game but it was strange the next morning when I woke up and heard on the radio that FIFA weren't happy."

JANUARY

Everton eased back into the winning groove by starting 2008 with a comfortable 2-0 success at Middlesbrough thanks to goals from Johnson and McFadden.

A 1-0 defeat to League One outfit Oldham meant Everton's FA Cup campaign was short lived. But the less said about that the better!

Instead supporters were looking ahead to the Carling Cup semi-final against Chelsea and despite Lescott's injury-time own goal handing Avram Grant's side a 2-1 first leg advantage, confidence was high that Everton could reach a first major final since 1995.

It wasn't to be though as Joe Cole's effort at Goodison saw the Blues of London through and the Blues of Merseyside, well, blue.

In the league Everton's points haul continued to mount. Lescott's sixth goal of the season inspired a 1-0 victory against Manchester City and Wigan, too, were put to the sword, a goal from Johnson and another for Lescott earning a 2-1 win and moving the Blues into the Premier League's top four.

The final game of January brought Tottenham to Goodison and although the Toffees offered more than enough to take the spoils they could not find a way through a stubborn Spurs rearguard. The result was a frustrating goalless stalemate.

Moyes moved to bolster his squad before the January transfer window slammed shut, bringing in two additions. Fleet-footed midfielder Manuel Fernandes joined the club on loan for the second successive season having failed to settle at Spanish side Valencia, and he was joined by Tottenham defender Anthony Gardner, who also arrived on loan.

The window also brought the curtain down on the Everton careers of James McFadden and Alan Stubbs. Faddy left to link up with former international boss Alex McLeish at Birmingham, while Stubbs joined Derby's relegation battle. The only other departure saw Brazilian Anderson De Silva make permanent his loan spell at Barnsley.

A brilliant goal from Yakubu gives Everton hope in the Carling Cup semi-final at Chelsea

Joleon Lescott's header finds the net at Manchester City

FEBRUARY

Everton played five times in February, winning four and drawing the other. It was form that culminated in a Manager of the Month award for Moyes, but in fairness it was probably recognition of Everton's fine form throughout the campaign.

The draw came in the very first game at Blackburn Rovers with the Blues drawing a blank for the second successive game. A goal glut was just around the corner however.

Phil Jagielka's header led to a 1-0 victory over Reading at Goodison, before a two-week gap in the Premier League allowed Moyes to concentrate on Europe.

SK Brann were Everton's opponents in the first knockout round with a tricky trip to the newly-crowned Norwegian champions up first. The Blues more than rose to the challenge and second-half strikes from Osman and Anichebe all but booked a quarter final slot.

This was duly achieved seven days later when Yakubu grabbed another hat-trick as Brann were trounced 6-1.

A return to domestic action meant a trip to Manchester City, one of Everton's top-half rivals. Once again the Blues delivered and goals before the break from Lescott and the in-form Yakubu fired us back into fourth.

MARCH

The opening fixture of March resulted in a hard-fought home win over another close rival, Portsmouth. Again, Yakubu was among the goals, scoring twice against his former employers either side of Cahill's seventh strike of the season.

When you come back down to earth though, it is often with a thud. And so it proved to be as a 2-0 defeat to Fiorentina at the Stadio Artemio Franchi gave Everton a mountain to climb in the UEFA Cup quarter-finals.

To their credit the players didn't let their heads drop and returned from Sunderland's Stadium of Light that weekend with a 1-0 win.

The return leg with Fiorentina ended in a 2-0 Everton win but after extra-time failed to provide a further goal, it was the Italians who progressed on penalties.

Three days later a header from one-time Toffee Brian McBride helped Fulham inflict our first league defeat since the turn of the year. Next up were West Ham, a team the Blues had twice beaten on the road in December, but who walked away from Goodison with a point.

Two poor results in succession had seen fourth place slip away, but March closed out with the Merseyside derby and a chance to put things right. Billed as the biggest encounter between the two sides in years, it turned out to be something of a damp squib.

It was settled early on by a Fernando Torres strike and after that it never really threatened to develop into an occasion that will linger long in the memory. More disappointingly a chance to finish fourth had all but disappeared.

APRIL

The visit of Derby, a side already doomed to relegation, appeared to present the perfect opportunity for a return to winning ways. But Paul Jewell's side had pride to play for and the Toffees had to battle their way to three points. Osman's sublime finish was the only highlight of a forgettable game.

A 1-1 draw at Birmingham followed as James McFadden squared up against Everton for the first time. The Scottish striker almost opened the scoring with a curling free-kick but it was his replacement Mauro Zarate who snatched a late point, cancelling out Lescott's opener.

Next up were title-chasing Chelsea and although Moyes' men showed plenty of

Another away win... this time at Sunderland thanks to this header from Andrew Johnson

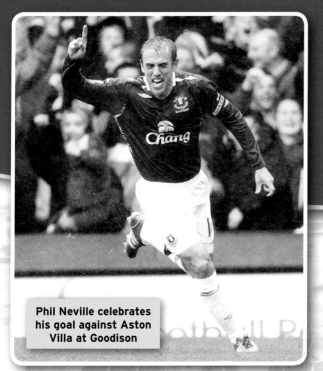

Phil Neville celebrates his goal against Aston Villa at Goodison

character it was the visitors' Michael Essien who grabbed the game's only goal.

Defeat threw the race for fifth wide open, with just three points separating Everton and their next opponents Aston Villa.

So often in football anticipation leads to disappointment but this occasion had it all – drama, tension, goals and a result which suited the Toffees. Twice Everton led – through the unlikely duo of Phil Neville and Joseph Yobo - but twice the visitors popped up to equalise - the last 11 minutes providing three of the goals.

MAY

The 2-2 draw protected the gap between the two sides and when Villa suffered a surprise home defeat to Wigan the following weekend it became advantage Everton.

A point at The Emirates Stadium would have all but ended the debate but Nicklas Bendtner ensured it would go to the final day.

The visitors were Kevin Keegan's Newcastle. Could Everton show the fight, the desire and the class that had earned them so many admirers throughout the season? Could they secure a second successive European campaign?

They did, emphatically, sealing a deserved 3-1 victory on an afternoon when they produced some of their finest football since the UEFA Cup exit to Fiorentina.

Yakubu reached the 20-goal milestone for the season to open the scoring midway through the first half before Michael Owen restored parity from the penalty spot.

A draw would have been enough for the Toffees but Lescott turned in his 10th of the campaign before Yakubu made sure with a penalty of his own 10 minutes from time…Everton's first Premier League spot-kick of the season!

Fifth place was safe - a just reward for the efforts of the players, manager, staff and supporters. The party could begin. A bright future beckons.

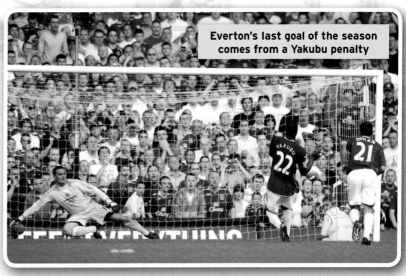

Everton's last goal of the season comes from a Yakubu penalty

Fixtures & Results 2007/08

THE PREMIER LEAGUE

March 2008						
Portsmouth	Sun 2nd 16:00	H	3:1	Yakubu 2, Cahill		33,938
Sunderland	Sun 9th 15:00	A	1:0	Johnson		42,595
Fulham	Sun 16th 13:30	A	0:1			25,262
West Ham	Sat 22nd 17:15	H	1:1	Yakubu		37,430
Liverpool	Sun 30th 16:00	A	0:1			44,295

April 2008						
Derby	Sun 6th 15:00	H	1:0	Osman		36,017
Birmingham	Sat 12th 15:00	A	1:1	Lescott		25,923
Chelsea	Thu 17th 20:00	H	0:1			37,112
Aston Villa	Sun 27th 16:00	H	2:2	Neville, Yobo		37,936

May 2008						
Arsenal	Sun 4th 13:30	A	0:1			60,123
Newcastle	Sun 11th 15:00	H	3:1	Lescott, Yakubu 2		39,592

UEFA CUP

1st round, 1st leg	Metalist Kharkiv	Thu 20th September 2007	H	1:1	Lescott	37,120
1st round, 2nd leg	Metalist Kharkiv	Thu 4th October 2007	A	3:2	Lescott, McFadden, Anichebe	27,500
Group stage, matchday 1	Larissa	Thu 25th October 2007	H	3:1	Cahill, Osman, Anichebe	33,777
Group stage, matchday 2	Nürnberg	Thu 8th November 2007	A	2:0	Arteta (pen), Anichebe	43,000
Group stage, matchday 4	Zenit St Petersburg	Wed 5th December 2007	H	1:0	Cahill	38,407
Group stage, matchday 5	AZ Alkmaar	Thu 20th December 2007	A	3:2	Johnson, Jagielka, Vaughan	16,578
Round of 32, 1st leg	SK Brann	Wed 13th February 2008	A	2:0	Osman, Anichebe	16,207
Round of 32, 2nd leg	SK Brann	Thu 21st February 2008	H	6:1	Yakubu 3, Johnson 2, Arteta	32,834
Round of 16, 1st leg	Fiorentina	Thu 6th March 2008	A	0:2		32,934
Round of 16, 2nd leg	Fiorentina	Wed 12th March 2008	H	2:0	Johnson, Arteta	38,026

FA CUP

3rd round	Oldham	Sat 5th January 2008	H	0:1		33,086

CARLING CUP

3rd round	Sheffield Wednesday	Wed 26th September 2007	A	3:0	McFadden 2, Yakubu	16,463
4th round	Luton	Wed 31st October 2007	A	1:0	Cahill	8,944
5th round	West Ham	Wed 12th December 2007	A	2:1	Osman, Yakubu	28,777
Semi Final 1st Leg	Chelsea	Tue 8th January 2008	A	1:2	Yakubu	41,178
Semi Final 2nd leg	Chelsea	Wed 23rd January 2008	H	0:1		37,078

Everton Ladies

This past year is one that will live long in the memory for Everton Ladies.

The 2007/08 season will be seen as one of the most successful in the team's history, with Mo Marley's side winning the League Cup and the Liverpool FA County Cup.

As well as their cup success, the Ladies secured a second place finish in the FA Women's Premier League, losing out narrowly to champions Arsenal.

The League Cup victory was made all the more sweet by the fact that it was the Gunners - unbeaten at the time in 59 games - who the Toffees produced an unexpected win against in the final.

After the victory the Everton Chairman, Bill Kenwright, spoke highly of the team: "This is a truly memorable and historic victory for the Everton girls.

"I know how much work they put in and they deserve everything they have achieved. I send the congratulations of every member of the Everton Board."

It was Amy Kane's strike on seven minutes at Leyton Orient that sealed the impressive 1-0 League Cup final victory over Arsenal and secured only the second piece of silverware in the club's history.

Manager, Mo Marley, insisted after the historic triumph that the victory was only the start of things to come for the Blues.

Everton Ladies celebrate
their cup success

Action from the FA Women's League Cup Final

"We knew it was going to be a hard game," she explained.

"Arsenal are a top, top team and you know that you're going to have to play out of your skin to even compete with them.

"I've always said that if our players have got the belief on the pitch then I think that we can be unbeatable. But our players have lacked that kind of belief over the years.

"I believe that we went into this game believing that we could win it and that is 90% of it. We've got the ability, but it's all about the belief.

"This is not the end; it's the start of big things for this club. We are now going to start winning trophies."

And how right she was - her side went on to lift the Liverpool FA County Cup just a few months later - beating city rivals Liverpool 5-0 at Goodison Park in the final.

A superb four goals from Fara Williams put the icing on the cake after a tremendous personal season for the Blues' England international.

The celebrations still didn't end there though. Two girls scooped awards at the 2007/08 FA Women's Awards.

A variety of accolades were handed out at the annual ceremony in recognition of achievements at both international and domestic level in the women's game.

Everton midfielder Jill Scott received the Players' Player of the Year while defender Fern Whelan was crowned Young Player of the Year.

Unfortunately Mo Marley was pipped to the post for 'Manager of the Year' by Fulham's Mark Saunderson.

Much is hoped for the Toffees in the 2008/09 season, with the Ladies once again challenging Arsenal to all the major honours.

Could this be the year that Mo Marley's side go that one step further and win the FA Women's Premier League?

A career in pictures
Tim Cahill

Tim Cahill travelled half-way across the world to achieve his dream of becoming a professional footballer!

He left his native Australia as a 17-year old to join Millwall and after establishing himself in the Football League he made the leap into the Premiership when he joined Everton in the summer of 2004.

Here, in pictures, are some highlights of his career so far...

Tim began his professional career in London with Millwall

Whilst at Millwall he played in the 2004 FA Cup final against Manchester United at the Millennium Stadium. Here, he is challenging Gary Neville

Tim has established himself as a big player in the big games and here he is scoring against Liverpool at Goodison Park

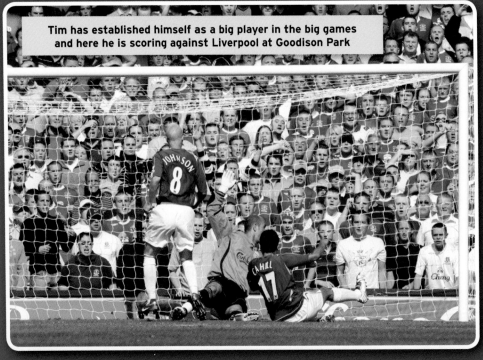

Tim's first goal for Everton came at Manchester City and he celebrated by pulling his shirt over his head...

...but the referee wasn't as pleased and Tim was promptly sent-off!

In 2006, Tim played for Australia in the World Cup and he scored their first goal in the tournament against Japan

A keen boxing fan, Tim's punches the corner flag whenever he scores a goal!

Dad's Quiz

1) From which club did Everton first sign Alan Stubbs?

2) Who scored Everton's goals in the 3-1 win at Tottenham last season?

3) Which club did Mike Walker leave to become Everton manager in 1993?

4) Who knocked Everton out of the UEFA Cup in 2005/06?

5) Against which team did Everton suffer their first defeat last season?

6) Who scored against Everton last season and later joined the club on loan?

7) Against which two teams did Yakubu score hat-tricks last season?

8) Everton's last defeat of last season was against which team?

9) During Walter Smith's reign as manager, Everton fielded three Swedish players in the team at the same time. Name them.

10) Who were Everton's opponents in David Moyes' first ever FA Cup tie as manager?

11) To which club did Everton sell Kevin Kilbane?

12) Which Everton player has also played for Stirling Albion?

Answers on page 61

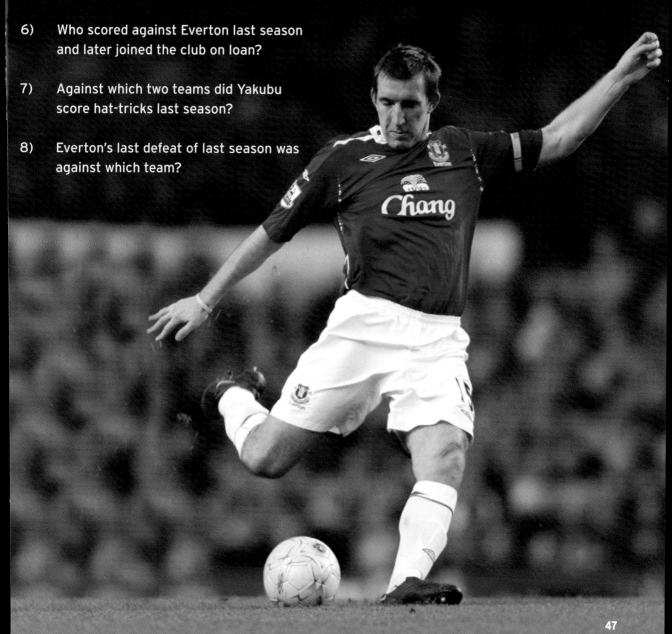

EvertonWay.com

WHAT IS EVERTONWAY.COM?
A detailed player development tool for players and coaches of all levels.

WHAT IS DIFFERENT ABOUT EVERTONWAY.COM?
We are the first Premier League club and probably the first in the world, to reveal our real Academy programme in the form of an online product. There are plenty of products on the market designed to improve football players and coaches, but none come from an established Premier League club like Everton. The results of our programme speak for themselves. Everton have produced a long line of players to feature in the Premier League over the years. To mention a few, Wayne Rooney, Richard Dunne and Francis Jeffers all graduated through Everton's Academy, along with more recent Everton first team players, Jack Rodwell, Leon Osman, Victor Anichebe and James Vaughan.

CONTENT OF THE SITE?
- The website uses video clips, diagrams, audio commentary and detailed supporting editorial to guide players and coaches through the real Academy programme.

- The programme covers every age

range in the Academy and breaks down the information relevant to 5-11's, 12-15's and 16-18's.

- The site replicates every department in the Academy and covers detailed information on Technical, Sports Science, Education & Welfare, Recruitment and Physiotherapy.

- Now anyone across the world can see real treatment sessions in the physio room, watch real Everton Academy practices and find out exactly how our young players train to be the best.

WHAT ADDITIONAL FEATURES ARE THERE ON THE SITE?

- A comprehensive development programme that includes full session guidance.

- A user forum to communicate with other users.

- Contact with real Academy coaches to ask questions with "Ask the Coaches".

THE SUCCESS

Since the launch of evertonway.com, the club has used this online coaching tool to engage with many football clubs throughout the world. The club has established strong links with grassroots football in India, China, North America and the Middle East and is being used to enhance the standard of football in these developing regions.

Who did I used to play for?

Have a look at these pictures of current Everton players in action for previous teams and see if you can guess who they are playing for at the time...

Answers on page 61

Phil Jagielka

Steven Pienaar

Dan Gosling

Mikel Arteta

Ayegbeni Yakubu

Joleon Lescott

Leighton Baines

Phil Neville

New kit photo-shoot

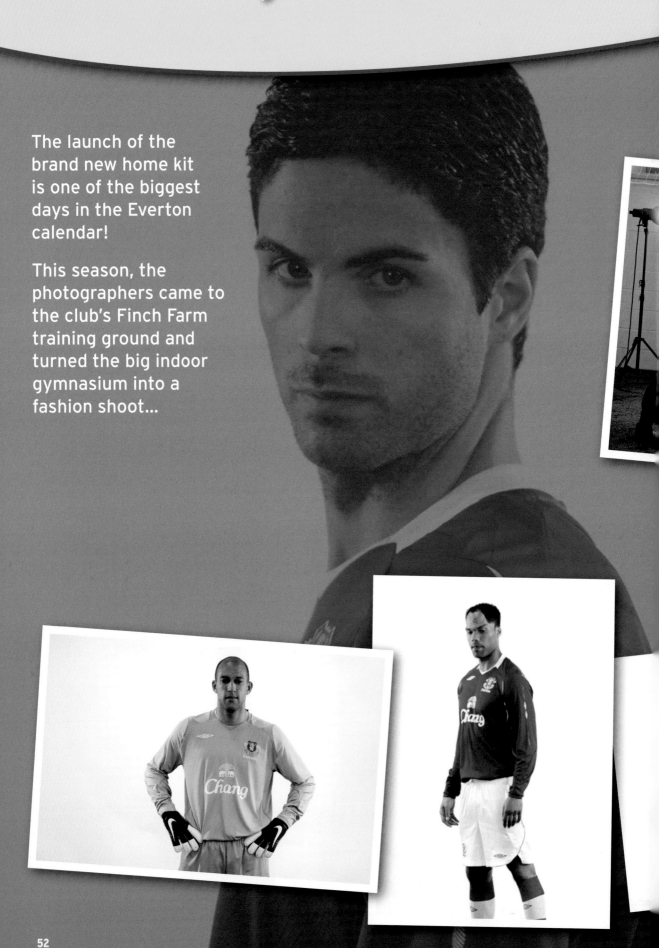

The launch of the brand new home kit is one of the biggest days in the Everton calendar!

This season, the photographers came to the club's Finch Farm training ground and turned the big indoor gymnasium into a fashion shoot...

evertonfc.com

evertonfc.com is the official website of Everton and offers everything an Everton fan could need.

The site was relaunched in the summer with a brand-new look, and is now better than ever!

It provides all the news associated with the Toffees, with new stories every day. The website is always first with the big news - whether it be transfers, match reaction or major club announcements.

The website team has unrivalled access to the players and provides loads of information on all of your favourite stars.

On matchdays, evertonfc.com is the only place to be if you can't make the game. The website provides extensive build-up, previews with the manager and players and a wide array of statistics.

Then, when the game kicks off, you can hear live commentary via our evertonTV service and monitor all the games going on around the country.

You can also see live photos from the match and then stay logged on after the final whistle for first reaction from the manager.

As well as this, there's a whole lot more...the website is home to plenty of interesting features about all things Everton, including our comprehensive UEFA Cup guide.

evertonfc.com is also home to a wide range of desktop wallpapers and screensavers which you can download, or why not pay a visit to eAuction, where you can bid on exclusive, rare signed merchandise.

Everton has an especially rich and fascinating history - and you can read all about it on evertonfc.com. We have a special dedicated section that charts the development of the club and provides plenty of information on some of the players that have contributed to its success.

The website is also the place to get all the ticket news, and you can even purchase match tickets online. There's also links to a host of services provided by the club for its fans.

If you're an Evertonian...you can't do without evertonfc.com!

evertonTV

evertonTV is the club's online television channel and offers a huge selection of video clips that subscribers can view whenever they like.

The library is constantly being added to with the very latest action and interviews from Goodison Park and Finch Farm.

evertonTV's cameras have unprecedented access to the training ground and regularly welcome the players and manager into their studio for exclusive interviews.

We were even on the pitch after the last match of last season!

The 3-1 win over Newcastle United secured European football again and as soon as the final whistle blew, evertonTV were on the pitch amongst the players, filming interviews as

they took their well-deserved lap of honour.

It's also the place to be to find a whole host of interviews with some of Everton's greatest ever players.

The likes of Alan Ball, Colin Harvey, Brian Labone, Howard Kendall and Graeme Sharp are all the subject of in-depth interviews as they discuss their impressive achievements with the Toffees.

evertonTV also has a wealth of archived match action. As well as highlights of every single first team game for the last three seasons, there's action from all the Everton games that have really mattered since the Premier League began.

You can also keep up to date with the reserves, academy

and ladies teams with their own dedicated channels.

Subscribers can also enjoy live commentary on a matchday and shortly after the final whistle, there's the post-match verdict of the manager.

European adventures have been a feature of Everton's fixture list recently, and evertonTV is there every step of the way. We chat to fans across Europe and capture the flavour of the local environment for those Evertonians who can't make the trip.

The service works out as a real bargain, with the price remaining at just £4.99 per month or £40 per year.

With fascinating new content being added daily, do you know what you are missing?

UEFA Cup

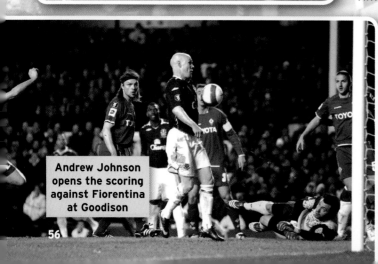

The scoreboard says it all! An emphatic victory over SK Brann

2007/08 was the season that saw Everton return to Europe!

A sixth-place finish in the Premier League had secured a UEFA Cup place for the Toffees and everyone connected with the club thoroughly enjoyed the roller-coaster ride that followed!

Ironically, the UEFA Cup adventure almost floundered at the First Round stage when the unknown Ukrainian team, Metalist Kharkiv provided the opposition.

The teams drew 1-1 at Goodison Park in the 1st leg but the story of the night was a couple of missed penalties from Andrew Johnson. It left Everton with a lot to do in the 2nd leg but a wonderfully spirited display over in Ukraine earned David

Moyes' side a safe passage through to the group stage.

Everton were grouped with AC Larissa (Greece), Nürnberg (Germany), Zenit St Petersberg (Russia) and AZ Alkmaar (Holland).

The 3-1 win in the first game against Larissa included the Everton goal of the season when Tim Cahill, Leighton Baines and Steven Pienaar created an opening from which Leon Osman blasted the ball into the net from 20 yards.

The trip to Nürnberg was truly memorable...even before a ball was kicked!

The German city was taken over by travelling Evertonians and there was a carnival atmosphere ahead of the game. The players didn't disappoint either, running out 2-0 winners thanks to Mikel Arteta and Victor Anichebe.

Zenit St Petersberg eventually won the tournament but in the group stage they found Everton too hot to handle at Goodison Park. Once again, Everton missed a penalty when Arteta blazed over but a typically opportunist goal from Tim Cahill earned another win.

The group stage was wrapped up in Holland when Everton fielded a weakened team (having already qualified for the last 32) but still had sufficient strength to defeat AZ Alkmaar.

The 3-2 triumph gave Everton a 100% group record and set them up nicely for a potentially tricky tie against the Norwegians of SK Brann. However, yet

Phil Jagielka dives in to score Everton's second goal during the 3-2 win in Holland against AZ Alkmaar.

Andrew Johnson opens the scoring against Fiorentina at Goodison

A night to remember! The teams enter the stadium in Nurnberg

another away win all but sealed the passage through to the next round. It was bitterly cold in Norway but Leon Osman and Victor Anichebe warmed up the travelling fans with second half goals.

The return at Goodison was a stroll. Everton rattled home half a dozen goals, including a hat-trick from top-scorer Yakubu. The final score of 6-1 gave The Toffees a resounding 8-1 aggregate win.

The last 16 tie was a mouth-watering clash with the Italian giants of Fiorentina. David Moyes predicted that the team chasing a Champions League slot in Serie A would provide Everton with their toughest UEFA Cup test thus far.

He wasn't wrong.

In pouring rain in the picturesque Italian city of Florence, nothing went right for Everton and they were soundly beaten 2-0.

The second leg on Merseyside was a night of unforgettable drama...but it ended in heartbreak for the Evertonians.

The atmosphere inside Goodison Park was absolutely magnificent as Andrew Johnson, from close-range, and Mikel Arteta, from outside the box, restored parity in the tie.

Neither side could add to the scoreline, and when it went to penalty-kicks it was the Italians who kept their nerve to go through.

Everton were out of the UEFA Cup...but what an adventure it had been!

James McFadden scores a vital goal in the thrilling match in the Ukraine against Metalist Kharkiv

Mikel Arteta in action on the night that Everton defeated the eventual Uefa Cup winners, Zenit St Petersberg, at Goodison.

International Blues...

Ayegbeni Yakubu (Nigeria)

Victor Anichebe (Nigeria)

Joleon Lescott (England)

Phil Jagielka (England)

Jack Rodwell (England Under 17s)

Quiz Answers

WORD SEARCH

JUNIOR QUIZ

1) Wigan Athletic; 2) Celtic;
3) Oldham Athletic; 4) Alan Irvine;
5) Physiotherapist; 6) England;
7) Birmingham City; 8) South
Africa; 9) Gwladys Street;
10) Sami Hyypia; 11) SK Brann; 12)
Sheffield Wednesday.

DAD'S QUIZ

1) Celtic; 2) Lescott, Stubbs,
Osman; 3) Norwich City;
4) Dinamo Bucharest;
5) Reading; 6) Anthony Gardiner;
7) Fulham and SK Brann;
8) Arsenal; 9) Tobias Linderoth,
Niclas Alexandersson and Jesper
Blomqvist; 10) Shrewsbury; 11)
Wigan Athletic; 12) Iain Turner

WHO DID I PLAY FOR?

Neville - Manchester United
Lescott - Wolves
Arteta - Rangers
Baines - Wigan
Yakubu - Portsmouth
Jagielka - Sheffield United
Pienaar - Ajax
Gosling - Plymouth Argyle

SPOT THE DIFFERENCE